Learning to PRAY

DEN SLATTERY

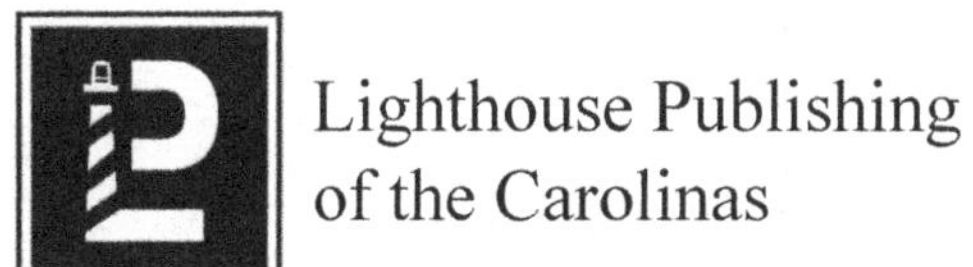

Lighthouse Publishing
of the Carolinas

LEARNING TO PRAY BY DEN SLATTERY
Published by Lighthouse Publishing of the Carolinas
2333 Barton Oaks Dr., Raleigh, NC, 27614
ISBN: 978-0-6158989-0-2

Cover design by: Karthick Srinivasa

The Prayer Hour Diagram is from *The Hour that Changes the World*, by Dick Eastman,
Chosen Books, 2002. Used by permission.

Library of Congress Cataloging-in-Publication Data
Slattery, Den.
Learning to Pray/Den Slattery 3rd ed.

Printed in the United States of America

Other Books by Den Slattery:
From the Point to the Cross (1992)
Essential Truths (1997)
Life Goes On (1998)
Essential Practices (2000)
Obeying Jesus (2009)
Changed By War (2009)
Transformed by Christ (2010)
How to Self-Publish Your Book (2010)
Holding Christmas (2010)
Selling Your Self-Published Book (2011)

Learn more about the author at:
www.denslattery.com

Table Of Contents

Introduction

Something happens when we pray. We may never comprehend it totally this side of heaven, but we know that in some mysterious way prayer connects us with God. Prayer ushers us into the realm of the supernatural where anything is possible.

The God who created us wants to be in communication with us, so He made it easy for us to talk to Him wherever we are— and without the need for batteries or satellites. Yes, there is a supernatural mystery to prayer.

If there is one thing you can take away from this book it is this—**God Answers Prayer.**

Prayer can calm our nerves, heal our souls, bring life back to our bodies, and even help us to find our keys. So join me as we journey together into the mysterious prayer zone where strange things happen. It is in that realm that we find God faithful to meet our every need.

This book is meant to be a basic guide to prayer. You could think of it as Prayer 101. May this book inspire you to draw near to God, so that He can draw near to you (James 4:8).

Why Pray?

"If God already knows everything, why should I pray?" Have you ever heard that argument? I have many times. So before we talk about the mechanics of prayer, let's deal with the reasoning behind it.

1. **It develops our relationship with God** (James 4:8). Just like talking helps people get to know each other, so prayer helps us to get to know God. During our times of prayer we grow in our relationship and draw closer to Him.

2. **God wants to work in co-operation with us** (Matthew 18:18-20). For some reason God has limited Himself by giving us this thing called prayer. As we pray, God goes to work. Does He need us? No. Yet He wants us involved.

3. **Through prayer we enforce God's rule over the earth** (Ephesians 6:10-18). It's sort of like a student running to the Principal of a school to inform him that his rules are being broken. Satan is running all over the earth trying to cause trouble, and we are there to stop Him by calling on God for help. Our prayers literally can change the world. Even in the Lord's Prayer we pray for God's Kingdom to come to the earth.

4. **God commands us to pray** (Matthew 7:7). Not only does God encourage us to pray—He commands it. James 4:2 tells us ***"You have not because you ask not."***

5. **Prayer helps us unload our burdens** (Philippians 4:6-7). It's a healthy thing to pray. Everyone needs to be totally honest with someone who not only loves them, but understands everything. Yet the only one who is like that is God.

Those are just five of the main reasons why we should pray, but I think they make the point. God wants us to pray. So, let's learn how to do it better following HIS guidelines.

Grace

When I was growing up my parents taught us to say grace before our meals. I wasn't sure why, but I did as I was told.

The word grace in the Bible comes from a word that means gift (charis). So I suppose my parents were trying to teach us that our food was a gift that we should be thankful for. To accomplish that task they taught us this prayer:

"God is good, God is great.
And we thank Him for our food. Amen."

My wife, Karen, was taught to pray:

"Come, Lord Jesus and be our guest,
And let Thy gifts to us be blessed. Amen."

There is nothing wrong with those prayers, but if I grew up praying it at every family meal and yet didn't know why I was doing it, then I'd say there was some disconnect somewhere. Some might say praying before meals is what civilized people do, but is that the best excuse we have?

Take a look at what the Bible says: ***"The Spirit clearly says that in the later times some will abandon the faith and follow deceiving spirits and things taught by demons. Such teachings come through hypocritical liars, whose consciences have been seared as with a hot iron. They forbid people to marry and order them to***

abstain from certain foods, which God created to be received with thanksgiving by those who believe and who know the truth. For everything God created is good, and nothing is to be rejected if it is received with thanksgiving, because it is consecrated by the Word of God and prayer." (1 Timothy 4:1-5).

According to those verses our food is to be received with thanksgiving. Thanksgiving is defined for us in verse five as prayer. These verses are also used to condone the eating of pork, lobster, rabbit, and all the foods the Jews were told not to eat in Leviticus 11 and Deuteronomy 14. We can eat anything as long as we pray over it. Our prayers and God's Word make everything fit to eat.

There are no magical words or special prayers we all have to memorize to make our food good to eat. God gives us the freedom to figure that out for ourselves. Yet I think He does expect us to be thankful for the food He provides.

I know there are some who want to argue this point by saying "My money bought this food, God didn't give it to me." Yes, but where did it come from? Does it just fall from the sky? No, someone had to grow it, and process it for you to have it wrapped up in nice little packages. So it may have been your money that bought it, but lots of hands were involved in preparing it. Be thankful.

Many people often forget about the hard working farmers out there fighting bugs, heat, rain, and frost to bring in a crop that we can consume. Yet some farmers might even say, "I grew this food on my own land, so what does God have to do with it?" Everything! Where does the soil, the sunshine, and the rain come from?

Then there are the seeds. Most farmers either buy their seeds or save them from the last harvest, but where do seeds really come from? God made them, and everything else. The seeds a farmer plants in the ground eventually become the wheat we use to make bread, cakes, pasta, and so many other wonderful things. Even if you have a huge garden of your own and you spend hours on it every day, you are simply co-operating with God to bring food from the ground. Therefore, be thankful when you sit down to eat your food because it really is a gift from God.

Bottom Line—God wants us to pray over our food realizing it all comes from Him.

Night-Time Prayers

Nights can be scary for kids who don't have a full grasp of the world they live in. When the lights go out and they can't see into the dark, they often get scared. I know I did. So my parents taught me a prayer that was first published in an English Primer in 1737. I'm not sure what title it was given, but I'm sure it probably came from a concerned parent trying to comfort their children in the dark of night. It goes like this:

Now I lay me down to sleep,
I pray the Lord my soul to keep.
If I should die before I wake,
I pray the Lord my soul to take. Amen.

That was a prayer from my childhood. I don't know how many times I prayed it, but it didn't mean anything to me. It was just a prayer I memorized, and then when my parents told me to pray, I repeated it back to them. I had no idea that God really wanted me to share my heart with Him—to reveal the cares and concerns I had.

God was very far away from me as a child, at least that's what I thought. We didn't read the Bible or pray about our real needs, we just tried to be religious by following what seemed right in our eyes. I guess you could say we didn't know any better. We did everything we thought we were supposed to do, which included going to church. However, we just didn't see the connection between church and real life.

When I became a teenager, I essentially became an atheist. My parents got a divorce, so we quit going to church, which allowed me to sleep in from partying on Saturday nights. I was into the occult, getting drunk, discovering my manhood, dating, and just living for pleasure. By that point of my life, I had given up on prayer as something for kids and old people. Besides, it didn't work anyway.

As I look back on it now, I realize how blinded I was. It would have taken something pretty drastic to change my mind. I didn't know it then, but that was exactly what God had in mind.

Bottom Line—We should pray before we go to bed thanking God for the day and asking for His protection as we sleep. Check out these verses.

Psalm 4:8—"***I will lie down and sleep in peace for You alone, O Lord, make me dwell in safety.***"

Psalm 92:1-2—***"It is good to praise the Lord and make music to Your Name, O Most High. To proclaim Your love in the morning, and Your faithfulness at night."***

Psalm 127:2—God ***"grants sleep to those He loves."***

Who Does God Hear?

I grew up in a middle class American family, yet I still found reasons to curse God every day. When I hit my hand with a hammer, stubbed my toe, or did some other stupid thing I blamed God for it. Cursing God and Jesus was so much a part of my everyday vocabulary that I did it without even thinking. At times, I would hold my fist in the air and curse God with a loud voice.

It's actually pretty strange for an atheist to curse the God he doesn't believe in. I mean, if there is no God, then who was I really talking to? Yet in spite of that break in logic, I persisted in that strange behavior every day. If there was a God, then everything was His fault.

But if I had known anything about the Bible or how God works, then I would have realized that God gives to all of us the freedom of choice and holds us responsible for our actions. Most of the things wrong with the world—crime, violence, rape, war, etc.—are actually caused by people who use their freedom of choice to hurt others. Our world is broken because we are broken. The things wrong in my life were the result of my bad decisions. God was just allowing me to do what I wanted.

Yet the idea of cursing God does get His attention. It says in the Bible, ***"You shall not misuse the name of***

the Lord your God, for the Lord will not hold anyone guiltless who misuses His name" (Exodus 20:7). So if God is going to hold me responsible for every time I misuse His name, then I am in BIG trouble.

People who curse God aren't exactly on His good side. Imagine if someone was publically saying very bad things about you, and then one day they came and asked you for a hundred dollars to pay a bill. Would you give it to them?

Now change that scenario to someone who talks to you every day and is a friend. If they came and asked for one hundred dollars, wouldn't you be more inclined to give it to them instead of the person who cursed you every day?

This seems like such simple logic, yet when it comes to God we think it doesn't apply. Consider these verses from Isaiah 59:1-2—***"Surely the arm of the Lord is not too short to save, nor His ear too dull to hear. But your iniquities have separated you from your God; your sins have hidden His face from you, so that He will not hear."***

So who does God hear? His family, His friends, and repentant sinners. I was none of those in 1968 when I joined the Marine Corps, but when I ended up in combat my whole perspective changed.

Bottom Line—God hears those who truly seek Him with a pure heart and are His friends.

A Prayer from the Heart

I arrived in Vietnam in the beginning of 1969, when the American military had around 500,000 personnel in country. I was in a Marine Infantry unit just outside of Da Nang. Every night we sent small man patrols out looking for the enemy.

The very first time I came under enemy fire I was behind a rice paddy dike, just hoping I didn't get shot in my first real battle. While men were screaming in the dark, and bullets were hitting all around me, some questions came into my mind:

Why am I here?

What happens if I die?

Is there a God?

I didn't know the answers to those questions, but I made a decision that night to start looking. That quest lasted several years. I looked into Eastern religions, the occult, and philosophy. I also asked other people my questions, but they didn't know either.

Then in 1972, I ended up back in Vietnam for a second tour of duty. When the rockets and mortars started falling those questions tormented me again and I was gripped with the fear of dying.

One night a guy handed me a Bible and told me

it had the answers I was searching for. I had discarded the Bible when I was a child because it was filled with "hithers" and "thithers." But that night I was challenged to open the Bible anywhere to find out how relevant it really was. When I did I looked at one verse and it changed my life. It is found in Proverbs 25:24—***"It is better to live in the corner of an attic than in a beautiful home with a cranky and quarrelsome woman."*** As soon as I read that verse I knew it was true and my arguments against God were decimated.

I started flipping the pages of the Bible and I found wisdom on every page. I was shocked. So I went outside and looked up into the dark sky and prayed my first real prayer from my heart.

"God, if You're for real, then prove to me that You exist and I'll believe in You."

The earth didn't rumble and there were no lightning strikes, but somehow I knew immediately that there was a God and that He had heard my prayer.

Bottom Line—God wants us to pray sincerely from the heart.

The Sinners Prayer

What is the "Sinners Prayer?" Some might describe it as the prayer Billy Graham prays after he has thousands of people come forward at his meetings, while the choir sings "Just as I Am." But where did such a thing originate?

Some people seem to think that sinners didn't start praying for God's forgiveness until the 1800's when Evangelists Charles Finney and Dwight L. Moody started doing evangelistic campaigns. They so easily forget many of the Bible stories where sinners cried out to the Almighty to have mercy on them.

Like the thief on the cross asking Jesus to remember him when He comes into His kingdom (Luke 23:42-43).

Or the tax collector in the temple who couldn't even look up to God, but just beat his breast as he cried out, "***God, have mercy on me , a sinner***" (Luke 18:13).

Or King David crying out "***Have mercy on me, O God***" in Psalm 51 after he had sinned with Bathsheba and killed her husband.

We are told in 1 John 1:9 "***If we confess our sins, He is faithful and just and will forgive us our sins and purify us from all unrighteousness.***"

God wants people to confess their sins to Him. It's what repentant sinners do to get right with God.

Whether we call it a "sinner's prayer," a "forgiveness prayer," or a "get right with God prayer," they all lead to forgiveness and mercy from the Almighty. God wants to forgive people. Just look at the Prodigal Son story in Luke 15. In that story God is the Father just waiting for the wayward son to return.

So if you have never asked God to forgive you for your sins, do it now. Confession knocks down the barriers between us and God. Jesus came so we could have fellowship with the Father, but forgiveness comes first.

Once I became convinced that God was listening to my prayers, I started reading the Bible with a new perspective. Yet as I read the Bible I discovered that God took a dim view of my lifestyle. Many of the things I did, God referred to as sin.

For example, the Bible said we shouldn't lie, steal, kill, have sex outside of marriage, misuse God's Name, serve any other God, or even desire things that other people have. Those who disobeyed God would come under His curse and have to face His wrath on Judgment day. Making that discovery led me to believe that I was in BIG trouble, because those things described me.

One night I felt so convicted for my sins that I just sat in my car crying. I wanted to get right with God, but I didn't know how to do it.

About a month later, I attended a Christian concert in Jackson, Michigan. The leader preached about getting right with God and finding forgiveness. So when he invited people to come forward and pray the sinner's prayer—I went. When we arrived at the stage we were asked to get on our knees and pray with the leader.

"Dear God, I come to You as a sinner. I ask You to forgive me for my sins. Jesus, come into my life. I open the door of my heart to You now. Save me, Jesus, and fill me with the Holy Spirit. I give You my life. Use me for Your glory. Amen."

As I prayed that prayer I didn't feel the earth move nor did I see any visions. Lightning didn't strike and I didn't hear God's voice. But when I got up off my knees, I was a different person. I had been transformed into a new creature in Christ. I felt clean inside and forgiven. Jesus had changed my life! The Bible describes this transformation in 2 Corinthians 5:17, ***"Therefore if anyone is in Christ, he is a new creation, the old has gone, the new has come."***

Bottom Line—God hears the cry of sinners who want forgiveness.

Bugged by Prayer

After praying the sinner's prayer and getting right with God, I wanted to learn all I could. My first lesson was on prayer with a guy named Ray who was assigned to help me.

We met at the same park where the concert had been and arrived just in time for the mosquitoes to have their bed-time snack. For the next 30 minutes Ray told me how important it was to pray to God every day. I could talk to God like a regular person and ask Him anything. At the end of the lesson Ray asked me if I wanted to pray for anything.

I said, "Okay." Then I bowed my head, closed my eyes, and prayed a very simple prayer, "Lord, we are down here trying to study Your Bible and these mosquitoes of Yours are tearing us up. Please protect us so we don't get bit any more tonight, in Jesus' name. Amen."

When Ray heard my prayer he tried to lecture me on how wrong it was for me to ask God for those kinds of things. Ray then rambled on for another 30 minutes. But as we got up to leave I reminded Ray that we hadn't been bitten by any mosquitoes since I had prayed that prayer. He thought of it as a coincidence, but for me it was a crucial lesson on the love of God and the power He has to back up His promises. He is never too busy to hear the sincere prayers of His children.

Jesus said, ***"Ask and it will be given to you; seek and you will find; knock and the door will be opened to you. For everyone who asks receives; he who seeks finds; and to him who knocks, the door will be opened"*** (Matt 7:7-8).

Do you think He really meant that or was He just fooling around? Because if He really meant it, then we can ask for anything—even for mosquitoes to quit bugging us.

Bottom Line—We can ask God for anything.

Doing What Comes Naturally

There is a real mystery about prayer. It is a very advanced form of communication. We talk to a God we can't see, and yet He hears us from heaven and answers. That's why I say prayer is entering into the realm of the supernatural.

Based on my experience, I believe prayer is something that comes to us naturally. It's almost like we have been pre-programed to pray. Even atheists often cry out to God when they are in danger. I know I did.

When I first became a Christian I was so hungry for the Word of God that I read the Bible for hours every day. I'd read for a while, and then stop to pray. Sometimes I'd pray while sitting, at other times I would get on my knees, or even fall on the ground with my face in the carpet. Praying just came as a natural overflow of my new relationship with God.

My prayers weren't written down or something I had memorized, they came from my heart. And with those heart-felt prayers came tears. God was doing such a deep work in my life that I began to see how terrible my sins were from His perspective. That understanding just opened the flood gates and I wept deeply as I sought

God's forgiveness and mercy. No one had to give me a lesson on how to cry before God, or how terrible our sins are in His holy presence. The Holy Spirit was doing a fine job of convicting me without those class sessions. I guess that is just another part of the mystery of prayer.

At times I felt so close to God that I could feel His presence, and my skin would often just tingle. Those feelings of the presence of God drew me closer to God as I tried to give Him every part of me.

Oh, what joy awaits those who enter into this level of fellowship with God.

Bottom Line—Crying out to God comes naturally for us when we need help.

Who Do We Pray To?

While prayer seemed to come naturally for me, I met some people who tried to confuse me on this issue of who to pray to. The Muslims pray to Allah, the Buddhists pray to their statues, the Hindus pray to millions of deities, and some Eastern religions teach that we should pray to our dead relatives. The Druids and witches pray to mother earth or the goddesses, and the Satanists pray to the Devil.

Then there are the Jehovah Witnesses who say we should pray only to Jehovah, the Jesus only folks who say there is no Father or Holy Spirit, and the Mormons who pray to a father god who is just a man that became a god. So who should we pray to?

Even among Christians there is a difference of opinion. For example, my Catholic friends pray to God, but they also pray to Mary, Jesus, and even a few dead saints. I realize the Catholics do that because their tradition teaches them to, but there is nothing in the Bible that tells us to do such a thing.

For years I served the devil, and at times even prayed to him. I knew there was supernatural power in the occult. Yet I have discovered that the God of the Bible, and Jesus His Son, are much greater than the devil or any demon from Hell.

So who do we pray to? I don't think it's wrong to cry out to Jesus, or even to ask for the Holy Spirit to help us. However, Jesus said in Matthew 6 that we should pray like this:

"Our Father who art in heaven,

Hallowed be thy name.

Thy kingdom come, Thy will be done,

On earth as it is in heaven.

Give us this day our daily bread

And forgive us our trespasses

As we forgive those who trespass against us. And lead us not into temptation

But deliver us from evil.

For Thine is the kingdom, and the power

And the glory forever. Amen."

The God we pray to is our Father in heaven. He has the power to forgive sins, to give us what we need daily, to guide us away from temptation, and to deliver us from the hands of the devil.

In the Old Testament God revealed Himself to people as the great "I AM (Yahweh)." He was also called many other names, but the most common was the "***God of Abraham, Isaac, and Jacob.***" Now we get to call Him Father.

Bottom Line—We pray to our Father in Heaven who knows, sees, and hears everything.

Praying in Jesus Name

Jesus once said, ***"I am the way, and the truth, and the life. No one comes to the Father except through Me"*** (John 14:6).

When I first became a follower of Jesus I would start weeping when I even heard the name of Jesus mentioned. Why? Because I was such a terrible sinner and Jesus is such a great Savior. To get right with God our penalty for sinning had to be paid by someone perfect and holy or we had no hope of getting close to a holy God. Jesus paid the debt He did not owe, so we could have the gift of eternal life that we did not deserve.

The writer of the book of Hebrews puts it this way—***"Let us then approach the throne of grace with confidence, so that we may receive mercy and find grace to help us in our time of need"*** (Hebrews 4:16).

But how do we approach God's throne? Obviously, we approach with humility and respect, but we come in the name and authority of Jesus who has prepared the way. Everything we have as Christians is because of Jesus, including the privilege of prayer. It's almost like we are saying as we approach our Heavenly Father, "God, Your Son sent me."

Jesus put it this way, ***"And I will do whatever you ask in My name, so that the Son may bring glory to the***

Father. You may ask Me for anything in My name, and I will do it" (John 14:13-14).

This is even better than the story of the man who finds an ancient bottle on the beach with a Jeanie inside who will give him three wishes. Jesus gives us His promise that He will make sure our prayers get to the Father even if we ask for a million things in His name.

So if we pray to our heavenly Father in Jesus name, and we do it according to God's promises, then we can be sure that our prayers will be answered. How cool is that?

When I discovered this secret I started praying about everything in Jesus' name and miracles started happening.

Bottom Line—We pray to our Heavenly Father in the precious name of His Son, Jesus.

Humility

In every religion when people pray to their god they approach that deity with signs of respect. That could mean they bow on their knees, fold their hands, close their eyes, or even lift their hands in the air as a sign of surrender. Many religions of the world also require that people bring a gift to their god. They do these acts to honor that deity. It's their way of saying that they think their god is greater than them.

The same is true of Christianity. When we come before God we try to humble ourselves out of respect. When we realize that the God of the Bible is the creator of all things—the greatest being in the universe and the most powerful—is it any wonder that to have an audience with the King would lead us to acts of humility? Look at what the Apostle James says about humility in James 4:6 & 10:

"God opposes the proud but gives grace to the humble. . . Humble yourselves before the Lord, and He will lift you up."

This doesn't mean we have to grovel in the dirt, although sometimes I think it's good for us to do just that since we came from the dirt of the earth in the beginning anyway (see Genesis 1-2). But humbling ourselves before Almighty God is an attitude of the heart which should affect how we talk to Him, as well as our body language. To rush into His throne room shaking our fist and screaming at Him doesn't really convey respect.

In the book of Malachi, God rebukes the people of Israel for not honoring Him with their gifts, money, marriages, and families. God was also upset with both the priests and the people for how they talk, and how they live in ways that show dishonor to Him. For example in Malachi 1:6 God says, ***"A son honors his father, and a servant his master. Then if I am a Father, where is My honor? And if I am a Master, where is My respect? says the Lord of Hosts to you, O priests who despise My name."***

The bottom line—God is worthy of our utmost respect. Yet how we approach God is also affected by the relationship we share.

Hats and Heads

Another sign of humility when we pray is to remove our hats. When I was growing up my mom would often take us to a Catholic church in Jackson, Michigan. I wasn't sure why we would go there in the middle of the week, but I guess my mom just wanted to pray.

Yet I noticed a strange thing when we entered the church sanctuary. My mom and two sisters had to wear a hat or scarf over their head, but I didn't. That seemed kind of weird to me, but I just accepted it as a tradition of the Church.

However, a few years later I developed a friendship with a boy my age that was Jewish. He and his dad both wore a hat or yarmulke (sounds like yam-a-ka) when they prayed. Yet when my family attended the protestant church no one needed to wear a hat. That just caused me to have more questions. Why do some people wear hats when they pray?

I once heard a Jewish Rabbi say that the reason all Jewish men wear a covering is because a Rabbi just decided one day that men shouldn't go around uncovered. That story appears in the Talmud, which contains Jewish traditions and teachings (see Talmud, Kiddushin, 32a). Another story is about Rav Nachman who wore a covering to remind him of the fear of heaven (see Talmud, Shabbat, 156b). Even today Jewish men wear a skullcap covering as a sign of devotion to God.

However, based on the New Testament men are not to wear a covering when they pray, but women are. Consider 1 Corinthians 11:3-10:

[3]But I want you to understand that the head of every man is Christ, the head of a wife[j] is her husband, and the head of Christ is God. [4]Every man who prays or prophesies with his head covered dishonors his head, [5]but every wife who prays or prophesies with her head uncovered dishonors her head, since it is the same as if her head were shaven. [6]For if a wife will not cover her head, then she should cut her hair short. But since it is disgraceful for a wife to cut off her hair or shave her head, let her cover her head. [7]For a man ought not to cover his head, since he is the image and glory of God, but woman is the glory of man. [8]For man was not made from woman, but woman from man. [9]Neither was man created for woman, but woman for man. [10]That is why a wife ought to have a symbol of authority on her head, because of the angels (ESV).

Those verses seem to indicate that a woman with long hair has a natural covering on her head, yet she should put on another covering for the sake of the angels. Perhaps they view it as an outward symbol of submission to her husband. Most modern women don't practice this anymore, but you will find it practiced among the Amish, Mennonite, and women in Middle and Far Eastern countries.

Christian men on the other hand should not pray with a hat on, which includes ball caps. If we do it says we dishonor our Head, who is Christ. (See Watchman Nee's book *Spiritual Authority*)

This whole topic has to do with honoring Jesus and submitting to His authority. Jesus submitted to the Father, and we are to submit to Jesus and to those He puts over us—which can include bosses, parents, husbands, spiritual and governmental leaders.

Bottom Line—Hats are made to protect our heads from the sun, rain, dirt and snow. However, when we pray our hats can either show respect or disrespect to Jesus. Christian men should not pray with their hats on.

Hands

When I was young and stupid I actually made my hand into a fist and foolishly held it up as I yelled at God. That is an example of how not to talk to God.

So what should we do with our hands when we pray? First, I think we need to realize that God knows us better than anyone and He wants us to come to Him as we are. Therefore, let me offer four suggestions:

Be who you are. Psychologists tell us that about 70% of communication is non-verbal. It has to do with the eyes, facial expressions, and body language. Most of us use our hands when we talk. God understands. I often use my hands when I pray.

Fold your hands. My wife often teaches kids that when they pray they should fold their hands so they aren't tempted to tickle their neighbor. That may not be your problem, but it just seems natural to fold our hands in prayer.

Lift up your hands. King David wrote, ***"Hear my cry for mercy as I call to You for help, as I lift up my hands toward your most Holy Place"*** (Psalm 28:2). Paul told Timothy, "***I want men everywhere to lift up holy hands in prayer, without anger or disputing***" (1 Tim 2:8). Universally, lifting up our hands symbolizes surrender.

Hold out your hands. Most beggars hold out their

hands, palms up, hoping for a gift. So it would seem to be culturally acceptable to pray with our hands out and our palms up and open.

Bottom Line—God gave us our hands, so we should use them when we pray.

Eyes

When I was growing up I was taught that we should close our eyes when we pray. Even now as an adult I often close my eyes when I pray. But do we have to close our eyes when we pray? Some of the obvious advantages of praying with our eyes shut include:

1. We can focus better
2. We aren't distracted
3. We rely more on our spirit

However, the mistake we make is to think that it is wrong to pray with our eyes open. What if you are driving a car and you get the urge to pray? Do you have to close your eyes? Or what if you are operating some machinery and you want to pray, is it really necessary to close your eyes?

The same argument can be made for those who think we need to get on our knees to pray. While that gesture is one way to show humility, it isn't required in every circumstance. Prayer is supposed to be a versatile way of communicating with the Creator of the universe—anytime and anywhere. One of my favorite ways to pray is walking around with my eyes open.

Consider some of the following examples from the life of Jesus:

"Then Jesus looked up and said, 'Father, I thank You that You have heard Me" (John 11:41).

"After Jesus said this, He looked up toward heaven and prayed, 'Father, the time has come. Glorify Your Son, that Your Son may glorify You" (John 17:1).

So do we need to close our eyes when we pray? You can if it helps you connect with your Creator. As for me—sometimes I do and sometimes I don't. In Christ we have freedom. The main thing is just to pray.

Bottom Line—I don't really think God cares if we pray with our eyes open or closed.

Getting Alone With God

When Jesus was walking on the earth 2,000 years ago, He would often sneak off by Himself to pray to His Father. For example, in Mark 1:35 it says, ***"Very early in the morning, while it was still dark, Jesus got up, left the house and went off to a solitary place, where He prayed."*** If Jesus did that, maybe we should too.

All of my Christian life I have been sneaking off to get alone with God. I'm sure some people think I'm weird, but to be honest, I like being alone with God. No one knows me better than God, and no one who knows me loves me as much as God does. How could God still love me when He knows all my secrets, my hidden thoughts, my failures, and my sins? I don't know, but to be truthful—it just baffles my mind.

If you want to draw near to God, you have to make time to get alone with Him. Now for those of you who may be new to the faith, that statement probably doesn't make much sense. How do we spend time with someone we can't even see? I mean, if we can't see Him we never know if He is there, right? Not exactly.

In Acts 17 the Apostle Paul described God this way—***"For in Him we live and move and have our being"*** (Acts 17:28).

And Psalm 139 says, ***"Where can I go from Your***

Spirit? Where can I flee from Your presence? If I go to the heavens, you are there; if I make my bed in Hell, You are there. If I rise on the wings of the dawn, if I settle on the far side of the sea, even there Your hand will guide me, Your right hand will hold me fast" (Psalm 139:7-10).

What's the point? We can't go anywhere to get away from God. That is true on so many levels. He fills the universe with His presence. He can be anywhere He wants to be at any time. He is with us when we are together with other believers (Matt 18:20), and He lives inside us. Remember when you came to Christ you opened the door and let Him in (Rev 3:20)? So we don't have to go looking for God, He is here and He wants to meet with you.

God says in His Word, ***"Let not the wise man boast of his wisdom or the strong man boast of his strength or the rich man boast of his riches, but let him who boasts boast about this: That he understands and knows Me, that I am the Lord who exercises kindness, justice and righteousness on earth, for in these I delight, declares the Lord"*** (Jeremiah 9:23-24). Those verses seem to indicate that God wants us to know Him.

And when Jesus was teaching His disciples how to pray, He said, "***When you pray, go into your closet, close the door and pray to your Father, who is unseen. Then your Father, who sees what is done in secret, will reward you"*** (Matt 6:6).

The "prayer closet" I believe can be anywhere that we can be alone with God. It could be on a mountain top, walking along a deserted beach, our kitchen, our bathroom, or it really could be a closet. I have prayed in many closets. The idea is to get alone with God, not to impress people with our act of piety. We get alone with God because we love Him and want to be with Him.

I remember one time I was at a conference with a bunch of people and yet my heart was crying out for God. But since there was no place to go, I went into a phone booth, closed the door, and pretended to be making a call, when in reality I was using my hotline to heaven, ***"Call unto Me and I will answer you and show you great and mighty things which you do not know"*** (Jeremiah 33:3).

When I was a student at Elim Bible Institute I would often sneak away to secluded places to pray. I still have fond memories of the furnace room in the basement of my dorm where I would go and pour my heart out to God. I always hoped that the furnace covered up my petitions with the Almighty, so others didn't hear.

Praying in places of worship when no one is around is also something I love to do. See if you love God, your time with Him is not a duty, but a joy. The Psalmist writes, ***"As the deer pants for streams of water, so my soul pants for You, O God. My soul thirsts for God, for the living God. When can I go and meet with God?"*** (Psalm 42:1-2). That has often been the cry of my heart. Is it true for you?

Bottom Line—God wants us to make time to be alone with Him every day.

Having a Quiet Time Plan

Christians often talk about having a quiet time with God. What they mean is a time for prayer, worship, and Bible study. I find that it helps to have a plan for that time.

The Bible was written one book at a time, so it makes sense to read it that way. At the very least you should try to read one chapter of the Bible and spend at least 5-10 minutes in prayer. Yet if that is all you do you may tend to look at it as a duty to be performed.

Nancy Leigh DeMoss has written a great book about having a quiet time with God called, "*A Place of Quiet Rest.*" She writes, "Devotions has become for me, not so much a duty (although there are still days when it is just that), as a delight—an awesome privilege to share sweet union and communion with the Bridegroom of my soul" (Pg. 16).

Some of Nancy's ideas on this time include reading the Bible, pouring your heart out to God in prayer, and even singing to the Lord. Whether it's some of the great hymns of the past or the worship songs of today, singing is one way to worship God, but it's not the only way. Some people make the mistake of thinking that worship=singing, which is not a correct interpretation. You can worship God by just sitting quietly before Him, or by just bowing down before Him.

Dick Eastman has a great heart for God. Many years ago he wrote a book called "*The Hour That Changes the World.*" The book is a guide in how to spend an hour with God. He includes a helpful diagram called the Prayer Circle (used by permission) which divides the hour into five minute sections.

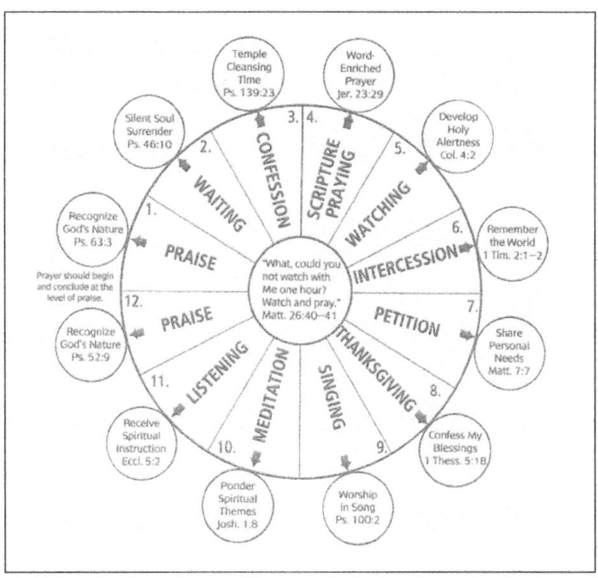

The idea is that if it's just five minutes you can do it. When I use this guide I don't always do everything on the list, or I change the order. Do your own experiments.

A simpler guide many Christians use is the acronym ACTS as a way to pray:

A= Adoration

C= Confession

T= Thanksgiving

S= Supplication

What I don't want you to do is just zero in on the methods and forget the reason for praying in the first place—to connect with God. We want to be with Him and get to know Him better.

One other thing I want to mention—God wants to speak to you. How does He do that? Let's take a look at that next.

Bottom Line—Having a plan for your quiet times with God does help.

Hearing God

Many people think prayer is just talking to God, but it's really a conversation between two people who love each other. If that's true then it shouldn't be a one-way conversation. What if God wants to say something to you? Do you ever give Him the opportunity?

The Bible is filled with stories of God talking to people. So why should it seem strange for God to continue that practice? Yet when God speaks to us it isn't just small talk:

God: "And how are you today, Den? Did you see the Michigan State game last night?"

Me: "No, Lord. I missed that one. Who won?"

When God talks to us, it's for a reason. God wants to communicate with us, but we need to get quiet and listen. Jesus said, ***"My sheep hear my voice"*** (John 10:27).

There are about a dozen Biblical ways God gets His message to people:

1. Angels
2. Dreams/Visions
3. Miracles
4. Prophecies/Prophets
5. Word of Knowledge
6. Voice/Still small voice
7. Nudge of the Spirit

8. The Bible
9. Circumstances/Opportunities
10. Preachers/People
11. Counselors/Friends
12. Things you read

The first seven of those may seem supernatural, while the last five seem more down-to-earth or logical. Yet I believe all of them are used by God at times in our lives.

However, if God really wants you to do something and not mess it up, He may send an angel, a vision, a prophet, or a magazine.

One day I was sitting at my desk going over a pile of mail that contained many training events for pastors. As I looked at the opportunities I prayed, "God, there are a lot of great opportunities here that I could take advantage of, but I need to know which one You want me to go to. Help me to know Your will."

In an attitude of prayer I grabbed each brochure and held it up to the Lord asking, "This one?" The answer I kept getting was "NO!" Until I finally hit upon the right one, and God gave me a "YES!" I looked at the advertisement. It was for the *Holy Spirit and World Evangelization Conference* in New Orleans. It was scheduled for the hottest time of the summer. I wasn't sure this was God. I knew my wife wouldn't like the idea either.

"God are you sure? Wouldn't it be better if I went to this conference on church growth in nearby Chicago?" Silence. I looked at the mailing again. "Lord, if this is from you I need YOU to work out all the details, including convincing my wife, and providing for me to go."

I didn't say anything to anyone for a few days. I have discovered that whenever I tell people God is leading me to do this or that, I usually receive criticism.

When I did reveal it to my wife, she said, "Den, it doesn't make any sense for you to go to New Orleans. Why don't you go to Chicago?"

"Karen, I know it doesn't make any sense, but this is the one I think the Lord wants me to go to."

"But we can't afford it."

I agreed with her, but ended our conversation by saying, "If God wants me to go, He will provide."

From that day on I prayed about whether this was God's will, and I got the silent treatment. I knew God had spoken to me, but like Gideon, I needed a sign. If I knew for sure this was His will then I would just move out and do it, but I needed to know for sure.

About that time I attended a *Good News Conference* on the campus of Taylor University in Northern Indiana. During a lunch break, I wandered through the library. I have a real love for books, and enjoy just browsing around. I went upstairs and walked into the magazine section. There were hundreds of magazines on display. I walked up and down the aisles looking at all the different kinds of magazines without touching any of them. As I came to the very end of the final magazine rack, one magazine caught my eye, so I reached over, and picked it up. As I opened it, there was a huge advertisement on the first page I looked at. As I read the words I was stunned. Printed in bold large letters was this message:

"JESUS WANTS **YOU** IN NEW ORLEANS!"

I closed the magazine and said to the Lord, "God, that's good enough for me. I'm going!" Once I committed myself to going to New Orleans all the details concerning the trip came together. This story reveals an important truth—once God speaks to us He expects us to obey.

However, people often ask—**How can I know when God is speaking**? There are many voices in the world all trying to get our attention. We hear things on TV, movies, newspapers, magazines, books, the internet, and our cell phones. Our friends and family are trying to influence us. And then there is the devil who seems to plant thoughts into our minds which he fires at us like arrows. So how do we distinguish God's voice in the midst of all that noise?

Bill Hybels is the pastor of one of the largest Churches in America—Willow Creek Community Church in the Chicago area. Bill says that almost every month someone in his church comes to him saying they are being led by God to leave their spouse for someone else. Is that the leading of God? NO! It's human lust or the temptation of the devil, but not God. The Bible says that God hates divorce (Malachi 2:16). So don't just trust your feelings—trust God and His Word!

Many Americans often end up thinking any connection with the spirit realm is okay. So in desperation they turn to:

- Séances
- Quija boards
- Astrology
- Tea leaves

° Mediums & Psychics

° Witches/warlocks

° Spirit guides

° Automatic writing

° Consulting the dead

° Asking statues or pictures for advice

All of these things are deceptions, tricks of the Devil to lure you into his trap. If you want guidance, don't go to witches, palm readers, or psychics. Go to the God of the universe in prayer. Through regular prayer and Bible reading we get to know God and then it's easier to know His voice.

For example, sometimes I'll hear a voice in my head telling me to do something. If I don't obey right away the voice swears at me and calls me all kinds of names. Would God do that? NO! Furthermore, if any voice tells me to do anything that is contrary to the Bible, then I know it's not from God. God doesn't change His mind or say something contrary to His Word.

How do we know God's voice?

Let me give you a list of things I look for.

1. Is it consistent with the Bible?
2. Is the voice harsh and demanding or loving and kind? Satan drives people to do things. God is loving and kind.
3. Is the voice condemning? Does it swear at you? *"You spineless hypocrite. You're nothing but a piece of trash."* God doesn't talk like that.

4. Is the voice wanting you to act quickly? Satan is in a hurry and doesn't want you to think too long about it. He wants you to act on desire and impulse. God is patient.
5. Is the voice leading you to sin or disobey God? God doesn't want us to sin and doesn't lead us into rebellion. In the Lord's Prayer we pray, ***"Lead me not into temptation."*** But Satan wants you to sin so he can mock you.

One final bit of advice—Trust God! His Word says, ***"Trust in the Lord with all your heart and lean not on you own understanding. In all your ways acknowledge Him and He will make your paths straight"*** (Prov. 3:5-6).

To acknowledge God is to involve Him in the process, and then to give Him the credit (glory) He deserves. This idea is so important that I want to look at it again in the next chapter.

However, as we conclude this chapter let me just say that God wants you to seek Him. I love this verse from 2 Chronicles 16:9 which says, ***"For the eyes of the Lord move to and fro throughout the earth that He may show Himself strong to those whose heart is completely His."***

Is your heart His? Do you want to hear from God and do His will? Don't you think He knows that? Get alone with God and ask Him to speak to you. He knows how to communicate with you.

Bottom Line: Learn to listen—God is speaking.

Praying for Guidance

As a new Christian I heard stories about how God can guide us, so I thought I'd try it. I started out with simple things—"God, should I go to this Church?" And then I'd wait for a response. In my mind I'd hear conflicting answers.

"No, you idiot that is not the church for you."

"Yes, My son."

At first it was confusing. Now I know that if the voice I hear is cursing me, calling me names, or trying to get me to disobey God's Word then I know it is not from God. I used to look for signs.

"God if you really want me to go to that church, then make this light turn green, NOW!"

If the light turned green I would go. It seems silly now as I look back on it, but in 1973 as a new Christian I was serious. I so wanted to do what God wanted me to do that I tried all kinds of things like that. Maybe that's why God tolerated it, and even used it to encourage me.

Gideon did the same kind of thing. God called him to lead a group of men to defeat the enemies of Israel. But he wanted to make sure God was really leading, so he put out a fleece. The conversation went something like this:

Gideon: "God, if this is really of You, I'm going to place this fleece of wool out tonight. If You really want me to do this, then make the fleece wet tomorrow morning and all the ground around it dry."

When Gideon woke up the next day, the fleece was wet and the ground was dry. Yet just to be sure it wasn't an accident, he asked God to reverse it the next night by making the fleece dry and the ground wet. In the morning it was as he requested. So Gideon did what God wanted, and God helped him to win a great military victory.

There have been many times in my life when I needed to know for sure that God was leading in a certain direction because the consequence of my actions would be huge. One of the biggest happened when I was an Active duty Chaplain at Ft. Hood, Texas.

In December of 1989, I was sitting on the couch alone after everyone went to bed. I was just praying about the future, when I sensed God telling me to get out of the Army and pursue a Doctorate Degree at Trinity Evangelical Divinity School. Wow! That was huge. As I sat there thinking about it, I decided it was so big that I needed some major confirmations, so I put out my fleece.

"God, if this is really You, You're going to have to make it all happen. I'm willing to do my part, but I need to know if this is really You. Show me that You're leading me by this fleece.

Help me to get out of the Army in July

Let me Pastor a church in Dowagiac area

Help me not to hurt my record

Help me get accepted into Trinity

Help me to get a computer before I go.

Help me to pay off one of our cars

Help me to get back into the 246 Armor

Lord, could You convince Karen?

Help Karen find two good friends?

Help my kids to find friends too

"God, I know this is a lot to ask, but we need some miracles to prove to us that this is really what You want us to do. Thanks, Lord. May Your will be done."

So what happened? Every one of those things on my fleece list took place and we got out of the Army. Praise God! He had proven to us that this was indeed His will. He wants to do the same for you. But you have to ask. God helps those who ask for His help.

I'd learned an important lesson having to do with Psalm 37:4, which says, ***"Delight yourself in the Lord and He will give you the desires of your heart."***

Bottom Line—God wants you in His will more than you want to be there, but when He guides you, He expects you to have the faith to move out. As you obey, He will guide you.

Prayer Lists

If you have been a Christian for any length of time and have attended a prayer meeting, there was probably someone there with a list. There is nothing wrong with using lists to remind you of who to pray for. But some people forget that prayer is not just giving our list to God.

Some people treat God like He is Santa Clause. Yet God is not Santa Clause. We don't just stand in line until it's our turn, then go sit on His lap, tell Him what we want, get a candy cane and leave. God wants more from us than that.

What does God want? God wants a relationship with you, not just a list of your requests. He cares about you and every detail in your life. He is your Heavenly Father who wants to mold and shape your life so that each and every day you become more like Jesus Christ (Romans 8:29). God has a plan for your life, and one of the ways He shapes us is through prayer.

Our needs and desires cause us to want to go to God in prayer. But when we get in His presence and start talking with the Almighty it does something to us. God starts changing our heart and speaking to our mind and spirit. That is why some people say—"Prayer changes everything." It changes us, it changes those we pray for, it changes our circumstances, it changes the spiritual climate, and it even changes our world. When we understand that, it helps us to see prayer in a whole new light.

Bottom Line: Prayer is not just about lists, it's about a relationship.

Keeping Track of Your Prayers

When I started discipling people one of the things I asked them to do was to keep track of their prayers. So when we had prayer concerns we would write them down on a sheet of paper and then post them on the refrigerator or the kitchen cupboards. Those pieces of paper sparked lots of discussion with their friends and family members. Whenever a prayer request was answered we would post the answer next to the prayer and date it. As soon as people started to see how effective our prayers were all kinds of people wanted to put up their requests.

One of the big problems Christians have is that we pray for all kinds of things and then just go about our daily life and often forget what we even prayed for. So when God answers, it just goes right on by without our notice. Yet if we keep track of the prayers we offer to God, as well as His answers, then I believe He is glorified and honored by all who know.

Another problem we have is that we think our prayers will only be answered if we "FEEL GOD'S PRESENCE." I have to admit that I like to have that sensation, but it doesn't always happen. And I need to add, if you don't feel God's presence that doesn't mean He won't answer your prayer. That's why I still like to keep track of what I pray for. Even years later, I find that it builds my faith. Try it and see what you think.

Bottom Line—Keeping a record of your prayers can build your faith and honor God.

Praying Scripture

Christians believe in the inspiration and authority of the Bible. We believe it to be the written word of God and therefore in keeping with His perfect will. So it should not be surprising that many Christians pray the very words of God's holy book.

There are four different ways that I pray the Scriptures. The **first** is to actually pray one of the hundreds of prayers found in the Bible. They can be found in both the Old and New Testaments.

Several years ago, Bruce Wilkinson published a little 100 page book on prayer that sold millions of copies. It was called *The Prayer of Jabez*. It's hard to find the story of Jabez in the Bible, because it's hidden in a long list of genealogies in First Chronicles. There are only two verses in the whole Bible on Jabez, so he doesn't seem very important. Yet it would be hard to convince the millions of readers of Wilkinson's book around the world, because they have been blessed in amazing ways just by praying this prayer.

You can find it in 1st Chronicles 4:9-10—"***Jabez was more honorable than his brothers. His mother had named him Jabez, saying, 'I gave birth to him in pain.' Jabez cried out to the God of Israel, 'Oh, that You would***

bless me indeed and enlarge my territory! Let Your hand be upon me, and keep evil far from me, so that I might not cause pain.' And God granted his request."

God seems very willing to answer this prayer. Don't take my word for it, try it and see what happens.

The **second** way I pray the Scripture is called pray-reading the Word. This involves reading a passage of Scripture and then praying it. Let me illustrate by using the first verse of the twenty-third Psalm:

"***The Lord is My Shepherd I shall not want.***"

"Jesus, You are my Shepherd. When You are my Shepherd I won't lack anything because You are leading and guiding me. Thank You, Jesus."

You can literally do that through the whole Bible. It was something I learned while attending a church in Washington D.C.

The **third** way is to pray for understanding. As a pastor I do this almost every week as I try to figure out not only what the Bible says, but what does it mean for us today. For example, Jeremiah 33:3—***"Call unto Me and I will answer you and show you great and mighty things that you do not know.***"

"God, Your word says I should call unto You, and You will show me great and mighty things. God, what do you want to show us? Teach me so I can teach your people."

Sometimes that goes on and on as I struggle with a text. It's what I call praying over a text.

The **forth** way is claiming a promise. There are hundreds of promises in the Bible that God has given us, and He stands behind them. I'd like to talk more about that in the next chapter.

Bottom Line—There are hundreds of prayers in the Bible that we should adapt for our lives and pray them back to God.

Claiming a Promise

Neal and Mari Hicks are missionaries in Japan. I was with them recently at one of my churches where they were asked to pray. Part of Neal Hicks prayer went something like this, *"Lord Your word says '***Give, and it will be given to you. A good measure, pressed down, shaken together and running over, will be poured into your lap. For with the measure you use, it will be measured to you.'*** *I ask that You do that for this church who has been so faithful to us with their financial gifts. Bless them, Lord. In Jesus name, Amen."*

This kind of prayer is Biblical and I can testify that God does answer when we claim a promise from God's Holy Word. It is important to note that we don't do this because God may have forgotten what He included in the Bible. That would never happen. But we do it because it glorifies God and exalts His Word in our prayers and in our lives.

There is another reason we claim promises when we pray—it has a way of building our faith. Faith needs both a target and some evidence of proof. Our proof is in God's character and His promises.

For example, let's say you need $125 for a bill that is due next Tuesday. The $125 is your target, with a deadline of next Tuesday. Can you trust God for it? Has

God proven Himself faithful? I think the answer to both questions is "YES!" If you agree then find a promise in God's Word to base your prayer upon. Let me give you a few options:

John 14:14—"***You may ask Me for anything in My name*** (Jesus), ***and I will do it.***"

John 16:24—***"Until now you have not asked for anything in My name. Ask and you shall receive, that your joy may be full."***

Matthew 7:7—"***Ask and you shall receive...***"

Matthew 18:19—***"Again, I tell you that if two of you on earth agree about anything you ask for, it will be done for you by My Father in Heaven."***

So when you pray about your $125 you should include one of those promises. It might go something like this: *"Lord, You know I need $125 by next Tuesday. I don't have that money, so I need Your help. Your Word says in John 16:24 that if I just ask in Jesus name that I will receive, so I'm asking. Please help me, Lord. In Jesus Name, Amen."*

That's claiming a promise, but you do need to meet the conditions, which we'll talk about next.

Bottom Line—God wants us to claim His promises when we pray.

Meeting the Conditions

Almost every promise of God has conditions attached to them. For example, "***That if you confess with your mouth, 'Jesus is Lord,' and believe in your heart that God raised Him from the dead, you will be saved***" (Romans 10:9). That verse actually has two conditions attached with the promise of salvation.

Confessing "Jesus is Lord."

Believing that God raised Him from the dead.

Therefore, we could say with assurance that if you meet the conditions, then you can claim the promise of salvation. The same is true for prayer.

Let's look again at the four promises of answered prayer from our last chapter. See if you can find the condition to meet.

John 14:14—"***You may ask Me for anything in My name*** (Jesus), ***and I will do it.***"

John 16:24—"***Until now you have not asked for anything in My name. Ask and you shall receive, that your joy may be full.***"

Matthew 7:7—"***Ask and you shall receive...***"

Matthew 18:19—"***Again, I tell you that if two of you on earth agree about anything you ask for, it will be done for you by My Father in Heaven.***"

In John 14:14 the only condition is to ask in Jesus' name. The same is true of John 16:24. In Matthew 7:7 the only requirement is to simply ask. And finally, in Matthew 18:19 the condition is to agree with another person on earth.

Hopefully you can see by these examples that God doesn't make it too difficult to meet the conditions. That's because He wants us to pray, and He is more than willing to answer. The Bible has hundreds of promises that God has given us that He wants us to claim so we can experience His goodness. We just have to meet the conditions.

Bottom Line—Meet God's conditions and He will move all of heaven and earth if He has to just to answer your requests.

Be Specific

My wife recently told me a story of a girl about four who went shopping with her mom. When they went down one isle the girl saw Pop Tarts and said, "Oh, mommy, I really want some Pop Tarts."

But her mom said, "I'm sorry honey but it isn't on our list and we can't afford it."

When they went down the cookie isle the little girl saw Animal Crackers and begged her mom to buy them. "I'm sorry honey, but I can only buy the things on my list."

However, the little girl was not done begging. "Mommy, please buy me some Animal Crackers and Pop Tarts."

"Honey, I told you I don't have any extra money for those things." Then with a flash of insight she added, "Why don't you pray and ask Jesus to give you some Pop Tarts and Animal Crackers?"

That night during bed-time prayers the little girl asked Jesus for some Pop Tarts and Animal Crackers. The next day a worker at their Day Care handed them a bag filled with Pop Tarts and Animal Crackers.

Stories like that are very encouraging. They remind us that God cares even about the little things. But they also remind us that we have to be specific about what we want when we pray.

General prayers are not very exciting and they require no faith. It's just a nice gesture. An example might be—*"God, please help the hungry and homeless in the world. Amen."*

While that is a nice thought, it is not specific enough to help anyone. It would be better to narrow the target. *"God, I met Joe sleeping under the bridge today. He's homeless and doesn't have anything. Would you please help him find some food and keep him safe while he sleeps? In Jesus name. Amen."* Now, that is a much better prayer because it zeroes in on a specific need.

People make these mistakes all the time. I once talked to a Pastor's wife who felt she couldn't ask for anything small and personal. In her mind God was only interested in BIG things—war, world hunger, the AIDS epidemic, etc.

When you pray—if you need a green cow, then pray for a green cow. If you need $15.45 then pray for $15.45. God wants us to be specific about what we want. If you don't know what you want, then try to figure it out before you go to the God of all the universe and stutter in His presence, *"God, I would like to a. . . pray for . . .a. . . well... You know what I need. Thanks."*

What kind of prayer is that? It's certainly not the kind of prayer that is going to be answered. Consider this promise from Jesus:

"Therefore, I tell you, whatever you ask for in prayer, believe that you have received it, and it will be yours." (Mark 11:24).

Question: Can you really believe that everyone in

the world will be fed today, or experience peace, or have all their needs met just because you prayed a general prayer to that effect? To be honest—I don't have that kind of faith and I doubt if you do either. But to pray for someone I know by name to have their needs met, well that is altogether different and I can have faith for that need.

That is exactly the kind of prayer we needed for my nephew's wedding. The wedding was held in Cincinnati, Ohio in June of 1997. At the rehearsal dinner I sat across from one of the bridesmaids who was very upset. The airline she traveled on had lost her dress for the wedding and she didn't know what to do. I suggested we pray. She was reluctant, not sure it would do any good, but finally agreed. We joined hands and I prayed:

"Lord, You know where that dress is. Help the airlines to find it tonight and get it to Rebecca in time for the wedding. In Jesus name, Amen."

The next day I saw Rebecca in a dress that looked similar to the other girls, but definitely not the same. About five or ten minutes before the wedding started her dress arrived. She changed and looked just as lovely as the other girls.

Bottom Line—Be specific. Ask for what you want—exactly—and trust God for it.

Praying with Thanksgiving

As a father of six children I can tell you that I like it when my children thank me for doing something for them. However, there have been times when they weren't thankful and I got upset. Why? Was it because they forgot their manners? No, it was because it revealed a heart that wasn't grateful.

Gratitude is an attitude of the heart. If we receive something from someone we should show that gratitude in some way. For example, if I take my kids to Disney World and spend over $500 in one day, I'm not expecting the money back from them as if I just loaned it to them. I just want them to be grateful. Jumping up and down, hugging and kissing me, and doing back flips would be nice, but even just saying "Thanks Dad. I had a great day." That would make me want to do it all over again.

Well, don't you think God would like a little gratitude some times? He is our Heavenly Father who delights to bless His children. One of the ways He does that is by answering our prayers. Shouldn't we at the very least say, "Thanks, God? You're the Best!"

Very early in my Christian life I started praying for things with thanksgiving. I based that on several Bible verses like this one:

"Do not be anxious about anything, but in everything, by prayer and petition, with thanksgiving, present your requests to God" (Philippians 4:6)

Now when I go to God with a request, I thank Him ahead of time as an act of faith. Let me give you an example of a prayer with thanksgiving.

"Heavenly Father, I need $550 to pay my rent by tomorrow. You know I don't have that money, but You do. Could You please release $550 to me by tomorrow? And I'll give You all the glory. In Jesus name. Thanks God. Amen."

Of course, when the money comes, you thank Him again. Manners are important, even when you are talking to the God of the universe.

Bottom Line—When you pray for something don't forget to thank God.

Importance of Faith

There is a story in the Gospel of Mark about a woman who was desperate. She had something wrong with her that caused her to bleed all the time. This had been going on for 12 years and she had gone to every doctor she could find, spent all her money looking for a cure, and ended up being worse off at the end.

Then she heard about Jesus—how he healed the blind, the lame, and even the lepers. A spark of faith rose within her and she dared to believe that there was still hope for her. She could see it in her mind and then she declared it with her mouth—"***If I just touch the hem of His garment, I will be healed***" (Mark 5:28).

When she found Jesus there was a large crowd of people around Him. But the woman knew this might be her only chance, so she pushed her way through the crowd, and then reached out and touched the hem of His garment. Immediately she felt the healing power flow through her body. Jesus turned and asked ***"Who touched Me?"***

The woman wanted to hide, but she finally came forward and told Him what had happened. Jesus said to her, "***Daughter, your faith has healed you. Go in peace and be freed from your suffering***" (Mark 5:34).

That is just one of dozens of stories that are recorded

in the Bible dealing with the importance of faith. Just read Hebrews 11, which is often called the *Hall of Faith*, because the whole chapter is about faith.

What is faith? It is one of the few words defined in the Bible. Hebrews 11:1 says, ***"Now faith is the assurance of things hoped for, the conviction of things not seen."***

According to that verse faith is both a conviction and an assurance based on the promises and character of God. So when we are hoping for something we should just believe that it will happen. Even though we don't see it manifested, we need to be convinced it is ours, and it will be. Yet the people listed in Hebrews 11 revealed their faith by their actions. By faith **Noah** built an ark, by faith **Abraham** moved into the Promised Land, and so on. Therefore faith is an action word, not just a feeling in your gut.

Faith starts out as a thought, then it becomes a decision, followed by an affirmation, and finally it moves to action. Something else you should know about faith is that it can grow over time.

Consider Romans 10:17 which tells us ***"So faith comes through hearing, and hearing through the word of God."*** What does that mean? The kind of faith we are talking about is not faith in the government or yourself. It is faith in God and His promises.

Now where do you think we might find God's promises? There is only one place—in the Bible. When we hear the Word of God—the Bible—it plants a seed of truth in our heart. If we zero in on that seed by meditating on it—thinking about it—that seed can build our faith in God and His promises. The more often we do that the greater our faith.

However, let me remind you that faith requires action. You have to put it into practice if you want to see results.

One day the son of a Pastor misbehaved so badly that he was told he couldn't go to the Sunday School picnic. Later, the Pastor felt he had been too harsh on his son, so he told him he had changed his mind and the boy could go. At that point the boy looked even more upset. So his dad asked what was wrong. The boy said, "It's too late, I've already prayed for rain." That's faith.

I've heard it said that if you are praying for rain you should carry an umbrella as an act of faith. I think they are right.

Consider the words of Mark 11:24: "***Therefore I tell you, whatever you ask for in prayer, believe that you have received it, and it will be yours.***"

So when we pray we have to believe that God is listening and that He will do what we ask. Notice I didn't say that God can do what we ask. There is a big difference between those two. We know that God can do anything, that's why we call Him God. But will He do whatever we ask?

For many Christians this goes into unchartered territory. We now move from what **we want** to what **God wants**. We call this God's Will. Let's talk about that next.

Bottom Line—God has given us the ability to believe and He expects us to use it when we pray.

Praying God's Will

In the Lord's Prayer we pray: ***"Thy will be done on earth as it is in heaven."*** (Matthew 6: 10). That part of the prayer seems to indicate that God's will is done in heaven, but not on earth, which is why we pray for it to be so. Our world is in rebellion against God, yet God keeps trying to bring us back. A great promise about God's will in prayer is found in 1 John 5:14-15:

"This is the assurance we have in approaching God: that if we ask anything according to His will, He hears us. And if we know He hears us—whatever we ask—we know that we have what we asked of Him."

Yet the question remains, what is His will? Trying to discern God's will can be difficult. I have struggled over this issue many times in my life and there isn't always a clear answer. Yet in most cases we can find clear answers in the Bible. (I wrote a book on this topic called, *How Can I Find God's Will?)*

For example, let's say you meet someone who you really like. Soon you are convinced that they are your soul-mate. But there is a problem—they're married to someone else. You go to God in prayer and ask for His guidance, but He seems to be very silent on your request. You try as best you can to explain the situation, as if God doesn't know it already. Yet all of heaven is silent. You're confused. You really want this new person in your life, so why won't God act on your behalf?

The problem is that you don't understand what God has already revealed as His will in the Bible. Just read Exodus 20:14 ***"You shall not commit adultery."*** Adultery means having an affair with someone who is already married. This kind of ignorance of God's Word happens more times than you can imagine.

So the first thing we need to do to discover God's will is to read His Word—from Genesis to Revelation. I have met so many Christians who have never read the whole Bible. How can God guide us if we don't look at the map He has provided? Some day we will all stand before God and He will say to us, "Why didn't you read my book? You had time for everything else."

Bottom Line—God hears and answers when we pray according to His will.

Praying for Healing

Does everyone get healed when they pray? NO! Some preachers teach that, but I'm not one of them. I have prayed for many sick people in the last 40 years, and amazingly some of them have been healed, but not all of them. There are many things about this that we just don't understand. Yet there are a few stories in the Gospels that help.

One day Jesus went to His hometown of Nazareth, but the people were offended by Him. Mark 6:5-6 says, ***"And He could do no miracles there except that He laid His hands on a few sick people and healed them. And He marveled at their unbelief."*** Was it that Jesus didn't have the power to heal? NO! It was just that the people didn't believe.

In another story (John 5), Jesus went to the pool of Bethsaida where people gathered hoping an angel would stir the waters and heal them. Jesus walked up to one man and asked, ***"Do you want to get well?"*** He had been sick for 38 years, and he was there at the pool, so the answer seems obvious—or is it? Many people use their sickness as a way to get sympathy or to get people to wait on them. Not everyone who even asks for prayer really wants to be healed.

But when I'm sick and I ask for prayer, you can know

that I want to be healed. The first time I did that still stands out in my mind as if it was yesterday.

It was 1973, and I was in Korea with the Army for a one year tour of duty. As a new Christian I didn't want to fall back into the worldly trap of going to bars and hustling women. But without Christian fellowship I was easy prey for the Devil. Some of the guys in my unit kept after me until I finally gave in. My one night fling back into the bar scene turned into an every night ordeal. I was sliding back into a sinful life style and didn't know how to stop.

At that time I became angry with myself for lacking the discipline to live for the Lord. I also got mad at God for letting it happen. I couldn't see how God could forgive me for going back to my old ways, so I didn't seek His forgiveness. Yet I was miserable. I knew there was a better way to live. I just didn't know how to do it.

The event that turned my life around came in the form of sickness. It started in the early afternoon as a sore throat and a fever. This was followed by a severe headache and an upset stomach. By 6:00 p.m. I was almost delirious with hot and cold flashes. It reminded me of a sickness I had struggled with in Vietnam, which produced symptoms similar to those associated with malaria. I was writhing in pain and praying for death to come quickly.

"God, I'm no good to anyone like this. If I can't live the Christian life here on earth in a way that pleases You, then just take me home. Either take me home or heal me . . . Jesus, help me."

As I prayed that prayer it seemed like the Lord stepped out of eternity and into my room. I could sense His presence at the bottom of my bunk. I cried out to Him, "Jesus, heal me." As soon as I cried out to Him I began to feel a soothing cloud envelop me. It started at my feet and slowly worked its way up my body bringing relief and healing. When it reached my head, my eyes closed and I fell asleep.

When I woke up the next morning I was fine. Since that time I have prayed for many people to be healed. Sometimes I see instant results, while at other times it may take a while. God doesn't heal everyone I pray for, but He does heal some of them. So I continue to pray and just trust God with the results.

Bottom Line—God still heals and works miracles.

Repetition in Prayer

In 1969, I was serving with the Marines in Vietnam. They had a program called R & R where for one week we could get away from the war to rest and relax. I chose Australia. It's a beautiful country that is very much like America. While I was there I spent most of my time in bars, drinking and hustling women.

Then in 1973, I became a Christian and felt so guilty for many of the things I had done that I wanted to go back and make amends wherever I could. It was then that I started praying for Australia. I asked God to let me go back, not to hustle women in bars, but to preach the gospel.

God didn't answer that prayer right away. As a matter of fact, I prayed for more than 25 years that I could go back to Australia and preach the gospel. And still I waited.

So how often do we have to pray for something? Is once enough or do we keep banging on heaven's door until it opens? Some preachers believe that praying more than once for anything shows a lack of faith. But praying more than once for something may also show that you really want this thing too. Sometimes we pray once and forget it.

Jesus offers us some insight in Luke 18:1-8:

And he told them a parable to the effect that they ought always to pray and not lose heart. He said, "In a certain city there was a judge who neither feared God nor respected man. And there was a widow in that city who kept coming to him and saying, 'Give me justice against my adversary.'

For a while he refused, but afterward he said to himself, 'Though I neither fear God nor respect man, yet because this widow keeps bothering me, I will give her justice, so that she will not beat me down by her continual coming.'"

And the Lord said, "Hear what the unrighteous judge says. And will not God give justice to his elect, who cry to him day and night? Will he delay long over them? I tell you, he will give justice to them speedily. Nevertheless, when the Son of Man comes, will he find faith on earth?"

In the Sermon on the Mount Jesus told His followers to ***"Ask ...seek...knock."*** But in the Greek it says, ***"Ask and keep on asking, seek and keep on seeking, knock and keep on knocking."*** The Greek text shows continuous action.

In the last 30 + years of ministry I have known many women who prayed for years that their husbands would be converted, and they were. I have also known parents who have prayed over and over again for their rebellious children to come back to God, and they did.

So did God eventually answer my prayer to preach in Australia? YES! And when I went it was in God's timing. After I preached there was a spiritual breakthrough and many people came forward for healing and salvation. It was an amazing night.

Bottom Line: It's okay to ask God for the same thing more than once. Persistence does pay off.

Praying Continually

There is an interesting verse in one of the Apostle Paul's letters that says, ***"Pray continually"*** (1 Thessalonians 5:17). How do we do that and still have a life?

I've always thought that means we should be in an attitude of prayer. It's sort of like walking around with a speaker phone that is connected to heaven. We leave it on and just carry on an on-going conversation with the Almighty.

For some people this may cause a problem. If they believe that you should always pray on your knees, or always close your eyes, or always fold your hands. It's hard to drive with your eyes closed and your hands folded. Yet we really should pray as we drive because of all the crazy people out there on the roads. But how can we keep praying and still do everything else?

Brother Lawrence lived in the 1600's and yet people still read about him today because he discovered how to practice the presence of God. He is called the singing pilgrim, but is best known today for a book of his letters called, *The Practice of the Presence of God.*

Brother Lawrence wrote, *"The time of business does not differ from the time of prayer, and in the noise and clatter of my kitchen, while several persons are at the same time calling for different things, I possess God in as great tranquility as if I were upon my knees at the blessed sacrament*" (Pg. 12).

I don't know that I have reached that point in my life, but I often am praying even when I am talking to other people. I may be praying for insight or understanding, but I keep in touch with God that way.

Bottom Line: Keep an on-going conversation with God throughout your days.

Praise

In Psalm 150 we read, ***"Let everything that has breath praise the Lord."*** What does that mean? To praise someone is to honor them, to speak of them in a positive way, and to thank them. God delights in our praises.

I have a friend named Merlin Carothers who has written a whole series of books on praise. Perhaps his most famous is the first one where he shared his own story. It's called, *Prison to Praise.*

Merlin went to prison for stealing something, but was set free to go fight in WWII. Shortly after that he was converted and exonerated of all charges. He went on to become an Army Chaplain, and a famous author. At last count he had sold over ten million books. Yet one truth you will find in all of them is that God is worthy of our praise.

Praise is not just singing a song to God, it could actually be saying the words, "Father, I praise You today for giving me a good night's sleep. And I praise You for this great food I get to eat."

For some insight on praise try reading through the Psalms in the Old Testament. They are filled with praise. You might also want to find one of Merlin Carothers books and give it a good read. He will teach you more than I can in one short chapter.

Bottom Line: God wants us to praise Him for all that He does, and for who He is.

The Prayer Cycle

I like diagrams if they can help to illustrate in a simple way what I am trying to say. That is why I created the following diagram which I call the *Prayer Cycle*. Let's take a look at it first and then I'll make a few comments about it.

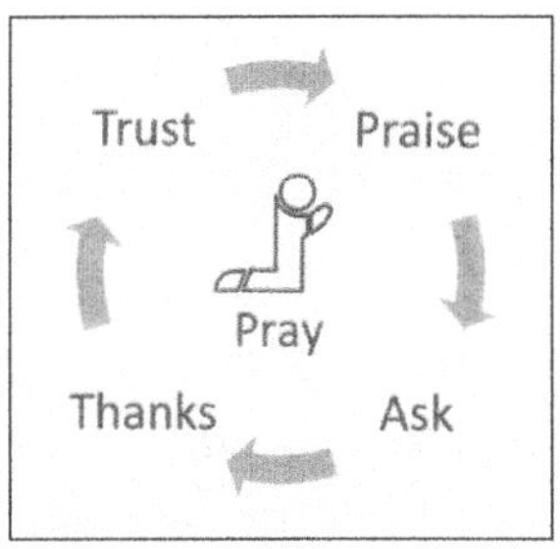

Humility

The Prayer Cycle shows that when we pray we should in some way humble ourselves before God. The Bible is very clear that ***"God resists the proud, but gives grace to the humble."*** (1 Peter 5:5). Whether we bow our heads, get on our knees, lay prostrate on the floor, or simply speak with reverence, there has to be some gesture of humility.

Praise

Then, like in the Lord's Prayer, we start with praise. "***Our Father which art in heaven, hallowed be Thy***

name." (Matthew 6:9). The word hallowed means holy. The Bible says in Psalm 100 to—***"Enter His gates with thanksgiving, and His courts with praise."*** It's as if we are entering the throne room of the greatest king in the universe. We enter humbly and with praise to the king.

Ask

Jesus said "***Ask, and it will be given to you; seek, and you will find; knock, and it will be opened to you. For everyone who asks receives, and the one who seeks finds, and to the one who knocks it will be opened"*** (Matthew 7:7-8). Then we ask for what we want, and we dialog with God about other things that are on our heart.

Thanks

1 Thessalonians 5:18 tells us to "***Give thanks in all things for this is the will of God in Christ Jesus concerning you."*** I like to thank God as an act of faith right after I ask Him for something.

Trust

Then we trust Him to do what He says He will do.

Bottom Line: When we have something to ask God we should do it with respect and humility, and then praise God—ask what you want—thank God—and trust Him with the results.

Final Thoughts

Prayer is an amazing form of communication that God has created for each of us to be able to go right to the top person in the universe. We don't have to wonder if our request will get lost or thrown in the trash before it makes it to God. He hears us when we go to Him as He directs. Jesus said, "***Ask and you shall receive; seek and you shall find; knock and the door will be opened for you***" (Matthew 7:7).

It's almost like Jesus has given us a blank check. We can ask for anything.

Too often we treat prayer as if it doesn't do much good, while in reality it connects us to God who holds the whole universe in His power.

Prayer is the mightiest force on earth.

Let me leave you with the words of the Apostle Paul from Philippians 4:6-7:

"Be anxious for nothing, but in everything by prayer and supplication with thanksgiving let your requests be made known to God. And the peace of God, which surpasses all understanding, will guard your hearts and minds in Christ Jesus."

Recommended Books

Prayer Works, Brother Andrew

Destined For the Throne, Paul Billheimer

Power Through Prayer, E. M. Bounds

The Practice of the Presence of God, Brother Lawrence

Prison to Praise, Merlin Carothers

Is That Really You God? Lorren Cunningham

Break Through Prayer, Jim Cymbala

Pray Big, Will Davis, Jr.

The Hour That Changes the World, Dick Eastman

The Navigator, Robert Foster

Too Busy Not To Pray, Bill Hybels

The Prayer That Heals, Francis MacNutt

Couples Who Pray, Rushnell & Duart

Psalm 91, Peggy Joyce Ruth

Let Prayer Change Your Life, Becky Tirabassi

Beyond the Prayer of Jabez, Bruce Wilkinson

Empowered by Praise, Michael Youssef

Den's Books

Transformed By Christ picks up Den's story where *Changed By War* ends. It tells how Den felt a call to the ministry and went on to become an Army Chaplain, and a Methodist Pastor. It is also a book about learning how to pray, how to hear from God, the authority of the Bible and much more.

The cost is $10.00.

Changed By War is the story of Den's experience in Vietnam. The war changed him as it does with everyone. This book has been called:

"Riveting"

"Inspiring "

"Life changing"

See what all the buzz is about by reading Den's bestseller, "Changed By War."

The Cost is $5.00.

Life Goes On could easily be called *Lessons from Life*. Each chapter tells a lesson the author discovered while living his life. It covers the years from about 1990 through 1998 with stories from Den's life.

The cost is $7.00.

Most of Den's books are available at www.amazon.com

For hard copies please send a check plus $3.00 for shipping t

659 Church St. Grass Lake, MI 49240

Den's website is www.denslattery.com

Made in the USA
Monee, IL
09 July 2022